CARDINAL JEAN-MARIE LUSTIGER
THE LORD'S PRAYER

(Translated by Rebecca Howell Balinski)

Our Sunday Visitor Publishing Division
Our Sunday Visitor, Inc.
Huntington, Indiana 46750

Copyright © 1988
by Our Sunday Visitor Publishing Division
Our Sunday Visitor, Inc.
ALL RIGHTS RESERVED

International Standard Book Number: 0-87973-493-0
Library of Congress Catalog Card Number: 87-62880

Cover design by James E. McIlrath

PRINTED IN THE UNITED STATES OF AMERICA

493

Contents

((1))

The unique model for Christian prayer

If we set out to search the gospels for Christ's teachings on prayer, we are likely to start from our own rather limited experience. To encourage ourselves, we look for situations with which we can identify. Noting, for example, that Christ withdraws from the crowds and spends the night in prayer (see, for instance, Luke 5:16; 6:12; 9:18), we do the same from time to time. Christ's participation in Jewish liturgical prayer at the synagogue (Luke 4:31; 13:10) and his institution of the Eucharist at his last Passover meal motivate our participation in liturgical prayer and the sacraments. Wishing to feel that Christ resembles us, we compare his feelings to our feelings: like us, he is exhausted by travel (John 4:6), overcome with grief when a friend dies (John 11:35), and shares the joy of a newly married couple (John 2:2).

We believe, as the Church teaches us, that Jesus, Son of God, true God and true man, was made "like his brethren in every respect" (Hebrews 2:17); that he has "in every respect . . . been tempted as we are, yet without sinning" (Hebrews 4:15). Just as Isaiah prophesied: "Surely he has borne our griefs and carried our sorrows" (53:4).

However, if we insist on understanding Christ by understanding ourselves, on grasping the meaning of his life by using our lives as reference points, we are not going to get very far in prayer.

* * *

If Christ has been made like us, it

is because we are meant to become like him. If he is our brother in sharing our humanity, it is because we are meant to become his brothers and sisters by sharing his divinity. If he subjected himself to our human condition, it is so that we can unite ourselves with him and, hence, become children of God. "For our sake he made him to be sin who knew no sin, so that in him we might become the righteousness of God" (2 Corinthians 5:21).

Christian prayer, therefore, does not depend on finding — even in the holy life of Christ — references to justify what we are doing. Rather, it is the act of allowing Jesus Christ to seize us by the hand and teach us to pray the way he prays. We can then let ourselves be led by him to a point where we would not otherwise dare to go. We can cross the threshold to a new existence which would have been inconceivable had we remained alone.

Jesus Christ is the way to a new life which he intends for us, the way to truth which he reveals to us by the Holy Spirit, the gift of Christ in union with the Father. Praying in the Christian manner means embarking on a lifestyle which is beyond imagination.

* * *

The "Lord's Prayer" is at the heart of Jesus' teaching on prayer. Why is it that these particular phrases — so terse and so beautiful — have been put on our lips by Christ? How can we make them apply to our personal needs and desires? If we project into each request that Christ makes the totality of all possible human requests, we are quickly disconcerted. Why, we may wonder, did Christ fail to mention a certain situation? Why *did* he mention another? The "Lord's Prayer" resists this kind of approach.

To our questions — possibly even to our objections — there is only one response: the "Lord's Prayer" is the prayer of Christ himself, his personal prayer: "He was praying in a certain place, and when he ceased, one of the disciples said to him, 'Lord, teach us to pray, as John taught his disciples.' And he said to them, 'When you pray, say. . .' " (Luke 11:1ff.).

Since Jesus passes on to us his particular way of praying, the key to understanding the "Lord's Prayer" is grasping what the words mean for Jesus himself. All the thrust of Christian prayer depends on our entering into Jesus' perspective when he prays to his Father and our Father (John 20:17). We must understand what Jesus understands, ask for what he asks for, give thanks for the things he gives thanks for. You may protest that such an attitude makes no sense, that it is, after all, *you* who are praying. Well, so you are. But *your* prayer, *our* prayer, every Christian's prayer, is the prayer of Christ.

The originality of Christian prayer is precisely that we share the personal prayer of Christ, as Paul reminds us: "Have this mind among yourselves, which was in Christ Jesus, who, though he was in the form of God, did not count equality with God a thing to be grasped, but emptied himself, taking the form of a servant, being born in the likeness of men. And being found in human form he humbled himself and became obedient unto death, even death on a cross. Therefore God highly exalted him and bestowed on him the name which is above every name" (Philippians 2:5-9).

((**2**))

A combat all the way to the cross

For the Christian, praying means becoming one with Christ. Hence, Jesus does not disassociate the invitation to pray from the call to follow him, "to walk in his steps." This Hebrew manner of designating a disciple is weighted with significance when the teacher (or rabbi) is Jesus! With him, there is no question of choosing to go in one direction or another, depending on the circumstances. When his hour comes, Jesus turns his steps toward Jerusalem with determination — a determination which shows on his face, as Luke points out in his gospel (9:51).

Following Christ, then, means going with him up to Jerusalem and remaining there to share his Passion. "We have left our homes and followed you," Peter recognizes (cf. Luke 18:28). Jesus, taking aside his twelve disciples, confides, "Behold, we are going up to Jerusalem, and everything that is written of the Son of man by the prophets will be accomplished. For he will be delivered to the Gentiles, and will be mocked and shamefully treated and spit upon" (Luke 18:31-32).

At Gethsemane, Jesus asks Peter, James, and John — the privileged witnesses to his transfiguration — to walk with him a distance beyond the other disciples, and when they stop, he says, "My soul is very sorrowful, even to death; remain here and watch." (See Mark 14:33ff.)

By his request, Jesus is associating these three apostles

with his prayer, which is a "combat" according to the primary sense of the Greek word for "agony" used by Luke (22:44). All of his being and all of his strength are engaged in this combat.

Christ asks the disciples to stay with him not so much for their support — since he "withdrew from them about a stone's throw," Luke tells us (22:41) — as to make it possible for *them* to follow *his* path, his prayer, and his obedience, a choice freely made but nevertheless painfully borne: "Abba, Father, all things are possible to thee; remove this cup from me; yet not what I will, but what thou wilt" (Mark 14:36).

* * *

The disciples fall asleep, and Jesus has to wake them. What are we to make of that? There is much more here than just a lesson, based on the apostles' weakness, on how we ought to pray. It is the occasion for Jesus to make a revelation full of mercy.

The disciples are overcome by the

torpor of the unbearable: not only physically but spiritually, since they withdraw into themselves and fail to "watch" during Christ's spiritual combat, a combat which characterizes all prayer. When Jesus finds them sleeping, he says, "So, could you not watch with me one hour? Watch and pray that you may not enter into temptation; the spirit is indeed willing, but the flesh is weak" (Matthew 26:40-41).

• The spirit? It is that fine point of our being which places itself in God's hands.

• The flesh? It is the condition of sinful men and women who, when it comes to offering their lives, to surmounting great trials such as the one Jesus faced, simply slip away from God's will for them.

Three times in succession the apostles surrender to their sleepiness, which simulates death. Jesus, alone, remains watchful in his combative prayer which results in his being able to face death and to conquer it.

And what about us? Jesus is no longer here to take us by the hand literally when, like the disciples, we balk at entering into his prayer. He is no longer here, but he suffered, died, and was resurrected, and has given us, children of God, the Holy Spirit who permits us to share his prayer.

The only truly Christian prayer is one firmly anchored in communion with the mystery of Christ and inspired by the Spirit who fortifies our wills to live up to what the Son of God, made man, wills us to do.

Paul writes on this subject to the Christians in Rome: "Likewise the Spirit helps us in our weakness; for we do not know how to pray as we ought, but the Spirit himself intercedes for us with sighs too deep for words. . . . When we cry, 'Abba! Father!' it is the Spirit himself bearing witness with our spirit that we are children of God" (8:26, 15).

It is the Holy Spirit who

transforms the Christian into another Christ. From the Spirit of the Father and the Son, we receive the strength to pray Christ's prayer, to say with him, "Thy will be done."

((**3**))

'His' prayer

Praying is something we are taught to do. Jesus was no exception. He learned the words and gestures of prayer from his mother, the Virgin Mary, and from his elders in Nazareth. The "Lord's Prayer" illustrates this fact beautifully.

When his apostles ask him to teach them to pray, Jesus gives them a prayer which is actually a summary of the Jewish liturgical prayers in common use at that time. It was standard practice for rabbis to make such summaries for guiding the prayers of members of their congregations. For his prayer, the rabbi Jesus borrows expressions from prayers he has been taught, but he shapes them into his unique prayer.

When we recite the "Lord's Prayer," we are praying with words that Jesus learned from his mother, Mary; words that express the faith of the people of Israel. Furthermore, since the Holy Spirit makes us similar to Christ, the only Son, we are praying in communion with his heart as he prays to his heavenly Father.

* * *

The major events of Christ's ministry — and, hence, his prayers — all take place within a liturgical framework and acquire a liturgical form. These events are at the center of Christian prayer and are found as such in the Church's sacraments and liturgy.

Across the centuries, Christian liturgy has been formed by a great diversity of languages, the expressions of many cultures. And it has never ceased to evolve with changing times. Nevertheless, all Christian liturgy remains faithful, to the point of "mimicry" as urged by Paul, to the traditions which were delivered to the first Christian communities (1 Corinthians 11:2). The Church structures its prayers by repeating literally the words and gestures of Christ, which are rooted in Jewish rites.

Today, we pray just as Christ prayed. Moreover, Christ continues to pray through our lips. The phrases of the Holy Scriptures, the word of God, must become a second "mother tongue" for all who are faithful to Christ. Moreover, the ritual gestures that Christ instituted and used to express his prayer must be inscribed in our sensibilities and memories as fundamental symbols of our Christian existence.

• For example, when the Eucharist is celebrated, we share the words that Jesus prays when he celebrates his last Passover. With his prayer, he seals the New Covenant because during the Passover rite, which unites the celebrants with Israel's exodus from Egypt, the Word of God made flesh offers his life beforehand as a sacrifice of praise to God. By his Passion and through his resurrection, his sacrifice will be received by God as a holocaust of redemption. Subsequently, Christians, through the Holy Spirit, will commune in Jesus' sacrifice by partaking of the sacramental bread and wine of the Eucharist.

• Jesus prays when he is baptized by John (Luke 3:21). The inconceivable depth of this mystical event is revealed when the voice of the Father is heard and the Holy Spirit descends upon Jesus, who is proclaimed as the beloved Son.

• Jesus prays at the time of his transfiguration in the presence of Peter, James, and John — who, a few months later, will fall asleep as Jesus prays in agony. Peter, alluding to the liturgy of the Feast of the Tabernacles, which was taking place at the time, remarks, "Lord, it is well that we are here; if you wish, I will make three booths here, one for you and one for Moses and one for Elijah" (Matthew 17:4).

• There are many other occasions in the life of Christ when he prays as he observes the liturgical tradition of his times and his people — from the weekly prayers at the synagogue to the great celebrations in the temple at Jerusalem.

* * *

If these Jewish celebrations and prayers have remained in the Christian liturgical calendar, it is because they refer us to the mystery of Christ. We celebrate Christ's celebration of these feasts, and he celebrated them in a manner unique to the Son of God. As Christians we celebrate the Jewish Passover, but it is the Passover of Jesus, observed just before his death. It is then that Jesus, Lamb of God who takes away the sins of the world, invites us to his wedding feast.

((4))

The mystery of the love between Father and Son

At a central point in the gospel — when the seventy-two disciples were sent out to announce his return — Jesus prays aloud. In order to understand what he is thinking and asking, we should pause and reflect on his prayer as recorded by Matthew: "I thank thee, Father, Lord of heaven and earth, that thou hast hidden these things from the wise and understanding and revealed them to babes; yea, Father, for such was thy gracious will. All things have been delivered to me by my Father; and no one knows the Son except the Father, and no one knows the Father except the Son and any one to whom the Son chooses to reveal him" (11:25-27). Luke says the same thing (10:21-22).

The evangelists point out that as he prays, Jesus "rejoices in the Holy Spirit." Every prayer to the Father, even in the holy humanity of Jesus, is an act of the Holy Spirit whose fruit is thanksgiving. Remember the beginning of the "Magnificat": "My soul magnifies the Lord, and my spirit rejoices in God my Savior" (Luke 1:46-47)?

Jesus begins his prayer by saying, "I thank thee, Father, Lord of heaven and earth" — in other words, "Creator and Master of all things." The resemblance of this way of addressing the Father to the phrase "Our Father who art in heaven" in the "Lord's Prayer" illustrates that their common source is the Jewish prayer of benediction and praise.

"I thank thee . . . that thou hast

hidden these things from the wise and understanding (the 'learned') and revealed them to babes," to those who have been "born of the Spirit" (John 3:6), that is, those who have been brought into existence by God so that they can truly become his sons and daughters. Hence, the importance of the word "Father" in this prayer of the only Son of God. Seeing his disciples as "newborn" is cause for Jesus himself to give thanks and to rejoice in the Holy Spirit.

"Yes, Father, for such was thy gracious will." With that statement of extraordinary consciousness, Jesus discloses the secret of God's love, which becomes visible to us in Jesus Christ, Son of God made man.

* * *

"All things have been delivered to me by my Father." This does not refer to "all things" which human beings can desire with a desire which is unquenchable and constantly in avid pursuit of more and more possessions and "happiness." Here the expression refers instead to the riches of the kingdom of God: divine life itself. Divine life is a total gift of life, freely bestowed; it is God and comes from God and has been received by Christ who receives *all* from God.

Jesus is the Son precisely because he does receive all from God. In his complete acceptance of "all things," are hidden the mysteries of the love and life of God's children called by grace to share in the divine conditions of the Son of God.

". . . No one knows who the Son is except the Father, or who the Father is except the Son. . . ." Jesus' prayer clashes head-on with our ignorance of God — our unbelief, our idolatry, the atheism of today and yesterday. But, by his prayer, Jesus himself is disclosing at that very moment who his Father and our Father is. He is opening up a domain otherwise inaccessible to man wounded by sin. It is the domain of God who is love and for whom we are made. Entering into the prayer of Christ means entering into the relationship which exists between Father and Son, between Son and Father.

". . . And any one to whom the Son chooses to reveal him." The Son does not choose arbitrarily, but benevolently with infinite love. All revelation of God is a gift; it is a sign and an offer of love made to those who pray.

* * *

I make this last point emphatically to spur us on. Each time that our desire to pray is aroused, it is Christ who, by his Spirit, is active in us. Christian prayer, far from being a difficult ascension, a heroic feat of hoisting ourselves by our own strength into otherwise inaccessible zones of spirituality, is rather a ground swell of love from Christ: love freely given so that we can share his communion with the Father.

Before addressing himself to the

Father and praying, Jesus has confided to his disciples, "I saw Satan fall like lightning from heaven." He is referring to the spiritual combat which crosses the hearts of men when they pray, and expressing his joy that the apostles have emerged victorious. Christ prays for all humanity so that through him, with him, and in him they, too, will triumph over the forces of evil.

Each time that a child of God enters freely and resolutely into the mystery of God's love, Jesus rejoices and gives thanks.

((5))

'Pray then like this:
Our Father. . .'

What are your feelings when you pray the "Lord's Prayer"?

• Do you ask yourself, "To whom am I speaking?" The sky seems empty, God is inperceptible. Does he hear? Does he even exist? And even though the fact that you are praying presupposes faith, do you wonder if your prayer is simply an echoless cry in the night?

• You are achingly aware that calamities — natural and man-made — abound, and that human suffering — in diverse forms — seems inevitable. What, you may be thinking, is God going to do about that? Is there any point in praying? Does any hope remain? If so, which one?

• Each day brings fresh evidence that the world is filled with hate and indifference. Do you feel despair over man's inhumanity to man? Do you question how human beings can love God whom they cannot see, when they have so little love for the human beings they do see?

Praying is definitely a challenge. In a world which has forgotten God, it tests our faith. In a world scarred by misery, it tests our hope. In a world racked by violence, it tests our love which must be strong enough to purify hearts that hate.

Jesus helps us to meet the challenge and overcome the painful obstacles to prayer by saying, "Pray then like this: Our Father. . ." (Matthew 6:9), and "not like pagans who merely repeat words, or hypocrites who wish to be seen." The disciples know that "the Father . . . sees in secret." (See Matthew 6:5-8.)

In the Old Testament, we read that at the three great feasts of pilgrimage, Israel went up to the temple in order to "appear before the Lord God,"* that is, to enter into the mystery of God. Christ's prayer places us squarely under the regard of the heavenly Father, and brings us into an intimacy with God which is altogether different from that experienced by the high priests of Israel who, all alone, reached him one a year in the Holy of Holies.

* * *

In order to speak to the Father, no one but Jesus says "*My* Father," or simply "Abba, Father" (cf. Matthew 7:21). But he adds, ". . . and *your* Father" (Matthew 5:16; Mark 11:25; Luke 6:36; John 20:17 — author's

---

*The use of the passive in the Hebrew and Greek texts attenuates the anthropomorphism: ". . . see the face of God."

emphasis). From that moment, the customary Jewish expression "our Father" becomes weighted with an original sense whose new depth Jesus will reveal to the apostles at the Last Supper (cf. John 14:17).

"I will not leave you desolate" (John 14:18). By the gift of the Spirit, Jesus will introduce us into the intimacy which he shares with the Father in heaven: we shall have God as a Father, and he will always hear our prayers.

"Whatever you ask in my name" (meaning as a son or daughter of God, in the name of the Son), "I will do it, that the Father may be glorified in the Son. . ." (John 14:13).

When we say "our Father," by the strength of the Holy Spirit who dwells in us, we become one with Jesus and thus share his filial bond with the Father.

But what about the times when, approaching prayer, we are confronted with the weakness of our faith, our

hope, our love; when we find ourselves
with an almost unbearable pain or else
a heart of stone? Is it not hard enough
to overcome such obstacles even as we
try to go about our daily activities?
How can we possibly overcome them in
order to pray?

• Our faith wavers: toward whom
does our prayer rise? First of all,
remember that when we say the "Our
Father," we say it in communion with
our brothers and sisters, with all
Christians throughout the world. But
also, and *above all*, we say it with
Jesus himself, our brother who gives
us the power to say *"our* Father" to *his*
Father. The words which we stammer
in darkness nourish the prayer of all
the children of God. Jesus, the only
Son, is with us as we pray, and he
struggles against the doubt and
infidelity of our obscured intelligence.
We are like Peter who, when walking
on the water, begins to sink. Jesus says
to him, "O man of little faith, why did
you doubt?" Similarly, Jesus takes us

by the hand and makes it possible for us to advance beyond the ordeal which paralyzes us.

• Our hope falters under the burden of misery and hardships which are humanity's lot.

Is God going to make things better? Isn't it too late? "Your daughter is dead," Jairus is told, "do not trouble the Teacher any more" (Luke 8:49). Praying to the Father is an act of hope which unites us with Christ our Redeemer, the Lamb of God who takes away the sins of the world, the Servant who takes all our suffering upon himself, the Word made flesh who in his agony at Gethsemane puts himself totally into the hands of the Father.

• To many of us, love seems to be the wildest of dreams, an illusion. By praying the words "our Father" we open up our hearts to Jesus' love for us, and we receive the grace to love the Lord our God and our neighbor.

((6))

'... Who art in heaven, hallowed be thy name'

> "Our Father who art in heaven..."

In conformance with Jewish piety, this "roundabout" expression allows us to address God without pronouncing his name, the divine tetragram revealed to Moses: I AM WHO I AM, which is the origin of the Israelite name for God, YHWH. "In heaven" specifies that God is not of this world, but *above* all the world; yet, he is our Father. Although human paternity cannot be confused with the heavenly paternity of the Creator, God is totally close to

the children he has created and called
to share his life. As Paul writes, he is
the Father "from whom every family
in heaven and on earth is named. . ."
(Ephesians 3:15). And according to
Matthew, human paternity takes all of
its meaning from our "heavenly"
Father.

* * *

"... *hallowed be thy name.*"

The use of the passive verb in
Hebrew is a respectful way of
designating God as *one who acts*. Each
of the requests of the "Lord's Prayer"
calls on God to act and seems, rather
audaciously, to be *ordering* God to act,
albeit according to *his* will. This
manner of praying is in marked
contrast to our personal prayers in
which we often "pour out our souls"
before God even though we believe
that the Lord "hast searched me and
known me" (Psalm 139:1) and recall
Jesus' reminder: "Your Father knows
what you need before you ask him"
(Matthew 6:8).

The "Lord's Prayer," however, is *Jesus'* prayer. It gives us the boldness to offer ourselves as obedient sons and daughters ready to participate in God's plan of salvation. Through Jesus' prayer, we submit ourselves to God's will so that he accomplishes in us what he wants us to contribute to his plan.

"Hallowed be. . ."

We ask God to hallow his name so that his holy action is accentuated. In Leviticus God says, "So you shall keep my commandments and do them: I am the LORD. And you shall not profane my holy name, but I will be hallowed among the people of Israel" (22:31-32).

On Sinai, the liturgy of the Covenant is both the revelation of God and the gift of his law, his commandments.

By asking God to hallow his name, we ask him to accomplish in us what he wants us to do. God the Holy (Isaiah's vision, 6:3) desires to communicate his holiness, the radical plenitude of life and love; thus, he gives us his commandments. When men and women obey God's commandments, they hallow God's name and God hallows his name when he allows those he has chosen to fulfill his will for them.

"*. . . thy name.*"

As I pointed out earlier, the "name" of God is what he revealed to Moses: "I AM WHO I AM" — that is, "I am he who is" (Exodus 3:14). The notion of God is not a category — *a* God who, *a* God that. God is the only person to have that name. He is the Unique One: "The LORD our God is one LORD . . ." (cf. Deuteronomy 6:4). Only God is God, as the Book of Nehemiah declares: "Blessed be thy glorious name which is exalted above all blessing and praise. . . . Thou art the LORD, thou alone; thou hast made heaven, the heaven of heavens . . . the earth and all that is on it" (9:5-6).

The mysterious name of God is at the beginning and end of his revelation to men. It will be understood only at the termination of history when we shall "behold the face of God" (Psalm 42:2). We shall see him who is, who brought us into existence and who is "with us" until the end of time. The expression "thy name" is then, as I said earlier, one of the numerous ways of speaking to God without pronouncing the four letters revealed to Moses.

* * *

The hope of holiness is at the heart of our prayer. It is neither a chimeric quest nor a presumption: "I'm going to become a saint!" It is an act of faith in God who is able to achieve his holy works in our sinful lives. When we pray, "Hallowed be thy name," we are saying, "You can hallow your name in the sinner that I am, in order to reveal yourself to all men, O Lord our Father."

It is precisely this role for us that the Lord announces through the mouth of the prophet Ezekiel: "And I will vindicate the holiness of my great name, which has been profaned among the nations, and which you have profaned among them; and the nations will know that I am the LORD, says the Lord GOD, when through you I vindicate my holiness before their eyes" (36:23).

((7))

'Father, I have revealed your name to men'

"Hallowed be thy name."

This initial request in Jesus' prayer heightens our awareness of both God's revelation and his calling *us* to holiness: he makes himself known to his children so that they become holy as *he* is holy. The holiness of man can be achieved only because God makes it possible for him to fulfill his will and share in his divine life. In transforming us, God is "hallowing his name" and completing his work of revelation.

It is in his Son, Jesus Christ, that

God fully reveals the glory of his name. In fact, only Jesus, who has come from the Father and is the Word of God made flesh, fulfills perfectly the will of him who sent him (cf. John 4:34). "I do as the Father has commanded me," says Jesus, "so that the world may know that I love the Father" (John 14:31).

Before Jesus' last Passover, ". . . among those who went up to worship at the feast were some Greeks. So these came to Philip . . . and said to him, 'Sir, we wish to see Jesus.' " Christ gives thanks to his Father for their request because he recognizes it as the first sign of the manifestation of God's glory to the pagans. That is why he prays aloud, "The hour has come for the Son of man to be glorified." (See John 12:20ff.)

By offering his life, Jesus proclaims the holiness of the Father "who did not spare his own Son but gave him up for us all" (Romans 8:32). Nevertheless, Christ trembles at this perspective of his Passion: " 'Now is my soul troubled. And what shall I say? "Father, save me from this hour"? No, for this purpose I have come to this hour. Father, glorify thy name." ' Then a voice came from heaven: 'I have glorified it, and I will glorify it again.' " To the astonished crowd Jesus remarks, " 'This voice has come for your sake, not for mine.' " (See John 12:27-30.)

Similarly, it is for our sakes that Jesus, addressing God the Father, gives thanks after the Last Supper: "I have manifested thy name to the men whom thou gavest me out of the world; thine they were, and thou gavest them to me, and they have kept thy word. Now they know that everything that thou hast given me is from thee; for I have given them the words which thou gavest me, and they have received them and know in truth that I came from thee; and they have believed that thou didst send me . . . and I am glorified in them" (John 17:6ff.).

God is glorified in Christ and Christ is glorified in his disciples if they do the will of the Father and exemplify — in the human condition and in spite of their sins — the divine power to love. "Love one another; even as I have loved you," Jesus commanded. "By this all men will know that you are my disciples." (See John 13:34-35.)

Therefore, becoming one with the Son as we pray his words to God, "hallowed be thy name," we are saying to his Father and ours, "Lord, you who make yourself known to us, who give us your law of holiness, we — your sons and daughters — entreat you that we may lovingly act according to your will for us. Let your holiness be reflected in us so that the nations shall know you (cf. Ezekiel 36:36). Called to be your children in the Son, we are 'a chosen race, a royal priesthood, a holy nation, God's own people' " (cf. 1 Peter 2:9).

When he "hallows his name"

through his children who ask him to do it, God is revealed to all nations.

* * *

Have you stopped to think about the full import of this assertion? We know all too well that we are sinners, that we are unworthy of being loved by God. And, yet, we dare to say, "Lord, we pray that your name be hallowed in us so that the world may believe that you sent your Son" (cf. John 17:21).

"Hallowed be thy name." What a breathtaking prayer! With those four words we welcome the revelation of the name of God *and* of his will for us. *Holiness* is our vocation, and holiness comes from God who sanctifies us by his Spirit. Therefore, we must pray constantly that God will continue to send us the Holy Spirit, the source of holiness.

When we pray in this way, we are expressing our trust that God will always act for his greatest glory and the salvation of all mankind.

((8))

'. . . Thy kingdom come'

". . . Thy kingdom come." It would be naïve to imagine that in pronouncing these words we are asking God to oversee the expansion of Christianity across the globe in the way that the president of a company striving to conquer the world market might do.

Remember the sermon of John the Baptist: "Repent, for the kingdom of heaven is at hand" (Matthew 3:2)? Later, Jesus, too, proclaims that the reign of God is "at hand" (Matthew 4:17). He sends forth his disciples to announce the news and gives them the power to accomplish signs which attest to it: healing the sick, raising the dead, cleansing lepers, casting out demons (cf. Matthew 10:7).

In order to clarify the apparent contradiction between the affirmation that "the kingdom of heaven is at hand" — which is a part of our faith — and the request of our prayer, it is important to understand just what the expression "kingdom of God" signifies. It refers to the time when God reveals that he is Master, the real king of the world who does not have to substitute himself for human sovereigns; then the hope of those who have believed in him from generation to generation is fulfilled, and the promise made "to Abraham and to his posterity for ever" is realized (Luke 1:55).

* * *

Just what are the specific ways in which the kingdom of God manifests itself?

The forgiveness of sins

Is it possible that we have simply grown accustomed to God's forgiveness? Why is it that our consciences seem so insensitive to the "heaviness" of our sins (cf. Psalm 32:4)? Is it all in vain that we have received the revelation of the holiness of God and the dignity of man who is called to share that holiness? Does the grandeur of the freedom which God has given us blind us to its fragility?

And, yet, surely we know that the evil that we do — against God, against our neighbor, against ourselves — cannot be "repaired" in the way that we "repair" material damages: sin provokes much more formidable consequences. Our evil deeds, our sins, are inscribed in our history from the moment we commit them. A wound is a wound; a betrayal, a betrayal; a murder, a murder; a theft, a theft; a lie, a lie.

It is God, and God alone, who can

pardon our sins. His pardon, however, is not to be confused with obliteration, amnesty, suspension of sentence, or even a reduced sentence.

God's pardon *re-creates* something which has been destroyed. Therefore, only the Creator can pardon, that is, *restore life*, to the man or woman who by an altogether sinful act of destruction has become a prisoner of death.

The resurrection of the dead

In the kingdom of God, death — "the wages of sin" (Romans 6:23) — is conquered. Death is the inexorable enemy of all human existence, the point of no return which no one who lives has experienced. (A person can feel that he is dying, but cannot *know* death.)

On this side and beyond our death, God, our Father, makes us become creatures who will live forever by the resurrection.

* * *

Both the forgiveness of sins and the resurrection of the dead are already works of the Spirit who dwells in us for our revival and sanctification. Moreover, it is the Spirit of God who makes it possible for us to live in faithfulness to him, according to his holy will.

* * *

Throughout the history of God's relationship with his people — first, Israel and, later, the pagan nations, as well — there have been spokesmen to express God's indignation over the suffering of the just, of those who are faithful to him, sometimes to the point of martyrdom.

When the kingdom of God arrives, the logic of the good, the true, and the beautiful takes over, and at the same time evil is exposed, denounced, and judged.

The kingdom of God is the triumph of the justice of God who dries the tears of the innocent and comforts the just: the love they have shown, the lives they have given have not been lost. On the contrary, they have become joy for God and salvation for the world.

The triumph of justice? A crazy hope, according to pagans; an illusion, claim nonbelievers. But, no. It is the kingdom of God, and it is coming. "And you shall know that I am the LORD, when I open your graves, and raise you from your graves, O my people. And I will put my Spirit within you, and you shall live. . ." (Ezekiel 37:13-14).

Finally, the kingdom of God also manifests itself by *the reign of God over the pagan nations*:

He makes wars cease to the end of the earth;

he breaks the bow, and shatters the spear,

he burns the chariots with fire!

Be still, and know that I am God.

I am exalted among the nations,

I am exalted in the earth!

— Psalm 46:9-10

((9))

*Before choosing and sending
the apostles to announce
God's kingdom*

"Thy kingdom come."

I have mentioned already that one
of the characteristics of the kingdom of
God for which we ask, hope, and wait
is his reign among the "pagans," the
"nations" who do not yet know God,
the Unique One.

Long before the time of Christ, the
question regarding the unbelief of
other nations was being posed to the
conscience of Israel: Why is God, the
Lord of the world, not worshiped by all

men? The conclusion was that pagans are prisoners of their idols; that their darkened intelligence and hardened hearts enclose them in their sin; that they are slaves of humanity's Enemy, Satan, who was homicidal from the beginning of our history.

God will cause his reign to come by delivering men and women from their powerlessness to know him. First, the hearts of the chosen people will be converted; they will become faithful and holy, just as Jeremiah says: "And no longer shall each man teach his neighbor and teach his brother, saying, 'Know the LORD,' for they shall all know me, from the least of them to the greatest . . . for I will forgive their iniquity, and I will remember their sin no more" (31:34).

Then, in the kingdom of God, *all* nations will accede to the knowledge of the true and living God and, in communion with God three times holy, they will share in the holiness given to Israel. God will put his Holy Spirit in them and "will take the stony heart of their flesh and give them a heart of flesh" (Ezekiel 11:19). When this happens, all people on earth will be able to live together in peace and mutual love because they will have a part in the Covenant that God destines for all humanity.

An insane hope? Not at all: it is God's plan. He will convert the hearts of all men and women, and the universe will be reconciled at last. Then, his kingdom will have come.

* * *

The name of God is hallowed when he reigns, that is, when he has conquered the familiar Enemy who enslaves each person and all of humanity.

The kingdom of God comes through and in Christ-Savior who accomplishes to perfection the hallowing of the name of God and liberates humanity from its prisons.

Note that the gospel (according to Luke, in particular) depicts Jesus in prayer at crucial moments in his ministry, at the moments when his request "thy kingdom come" takes shape in a way.

For example, Jesus spends the night in prayer before calling his disciples together and choosing the Twelve (cf. Luke 6:12-16) who are sent out to announce the good news: "The kingdom of heaven is at hand" (Matthew 3:2; see also Luke 9:2). Why does he pray? Because the Twelve are given to him by the Father, as he says in the Gospel of John: "And now I am no more in the world, but they are in the world, and I am coming to thee. Holy Father, keep them in thy name, which thou hast given me, that they may be one, even as we are one. While I was with them, I kept them in thy name, which thou hast given me; I have guarded them, and none of them is lost but the son of perdition, that the scripture might be fulfilled" (17:11-12).

By choosing his disciples in

prayer, Jesus receives them from the heavenly Father.

His disciples, in turn, are going to participate in the coming of God's kingdom by announcing it, on the word of the Son, by the power of the Holy Spirit.

"Thy kingdom come" is a request which disconcerts us owing to the fact that the request itself can be made only because the reign of God is *already* here. It fulfills the promise of the kingdom "not-yet-here," since the kingdom comes at the very moment when the Spirit of Jesus puts the words on our lips and unites us with Christ, who is *himself*, in his person, the kingdom of God.

« 10 »

God's kingdom comes when. . .

Jesus names Peter as the head of the twelve apostles who are sent out to announce the kingdom of God. The day before he gives himself up to his Passion, Jesus says to him, "Simon, Simon, . . . I have prayed for you that your faith may not fail; and when you have turned again, strengthen your brethren" (Luke 22:31-32). Christ prays for Peter and he prays that God's kingdom will come. In fact, these two intentions make only one.

Similarly, the gospel permits us to perceive in the words and gestures of

Jesus in his earlier ministry that his prayer to the Father asking that "thy kingdom come" is at the same time his thanksgiving for the fact that the kingdom *has* come. For example:

• When Jesus forgives the sins of the paralyzed man, who has been let down through the roof, and causes him to rise and walk (cf. Luke 5:18-25).

• When he raises the dead, prophesying his own resurrection. Standing before the tomb of his friend Lazarus, Jesus prays, "Father, I thank thee that thou hast heard me. I knew that thou hearest me always, but I have said this on account of the people standing by, that they may believe that thou didst send me" (John 11:41-42).

• When he asks the Father to send the Holy Spirit: "And I will pray the Father, and he will give you another Counselor, to be with you for ever" (John 14:16).

• When, through his Passion, he is subjected to the scandal of evil and endures the suffering of the innocent victim: "I have a baptism to be baptized with; and how I am constrained until it is accomplished!" (Luke 12:50).

• When the pagans discover God, the beginning of "the white harvest" (cf. John 4:35).

Otherwise, Jesus' parables about the kingdom of God disclose what he is asking for when he prays, "Thy kingdom come": he is thinking of the hidden germination of the word of God, buried now but destined to bear fruit later; he is also thinking of the good seeds having been mixed with the weeds of evil throughout human history.

Finally, when Jesus prays for the coming of the reign of God, he is looking ahead to his Passion: the "baptism to be baptized with" (Luke 12:50); the "cup" which he must drink (Luke 22:42) until he says on the cross, "I thirst" (John 19:28) and, finally, "It is finished" (John 19:30).

The disciples nurture the memory of Christ's patient hope of the Father's kingdom to which he invites them before his death: "I tell you I shall not drink again of this fruit of the vine until that day when I drink it new with you in my Father's kingdom" (Matthew 26:29).

When that day comes, the promise of the kingdom of God will be entirely fulfilled: all the multitudes of humanity will be completely reconciled in the blood of the Covenant and, to paraphrase Paul (Ephesians 1:10), all things in heaven and earth will be united in Christ.

As we await this day, Jesus — according to his last words to the disciples — is "with us always, to the close of the age" (cf. Matthew 28:20). We have everything to receive from Christ, our Head (cf. Colossians 1:17-18), and everything to look forward to. The kingdom of God comes again and again, but we must always pray that it will continue coming until

the end of human history when Christ
will be "all and in all" (Colossians 3:11).

* * *

"Thy kingdom comes, Lord. . .

. . . when, thanks to your Spirit, men
and women in all conditions and all
ages receive your word: 'The
kingdom of God is at hand; hear
the Good News,' and go about
repeating it to their brothers and
sisters;

. . . when any one of us confesses his
sin and receives God's forgiveness
in the sacrament of the Church,
thus experiencing and sharing the
grace of reconciliation;

. . . when we receive the gift of the
Spirit who makes it possible for us
to live in communion with God,
and to pass on, to *every* neighbor,
the love with which we are loved by
him;

. . . when Christ unites us with the
mystery of his cross and gives us

the hope of resurrection which will triumph over all sin and all evil: 'Then the righteous will shine like the sun in the kingdom of their Father' (Matthew 13:43)."

At the very instant that our lips are praying, "Father, thy kingdom come," the Spirit brings his kingdom into our hearts — because Christ is transforming us, and he never ceases to come to us or to have us come to him.

« 11 »

'. . . Thy will be done on earth as it is in heaven'

It often happens that this request is expressed as a resigned acceptance of an ordeal. Jesus' prayer during his agony at Gethsemane immediately comes to mind: "Father . . . not as I will, but as you will." In this instance, Jesus is submitting his personal will to that of his Father, offering his existence for the salvation of his brothers and sisters while all his being is plunged into dread and an abysmal struggle against sin — until "his sweat became like great drops of blood falling down upon the ground" (Luke 22:44).

But has it occurred to you that the Virgin Mary prayed the same kind of prayer in her secret joy at the Annunciation? "Let it be to me according to your word" (Luke 1:38).

The gospel leads us to discover that the same spiritual attitude can exist in two opposing situations.

* * *

". . . on earth as it is in heaven."

There are two ways of interpreting the word "heaven." According to the first, it means "the place where God lives" or "God himself," as when we say, "Our Father, who art in heaven." But we realize right away that this interpretation does not apply to the second mention of heaven in the "Lord's Prayer" because we would not be asking God to accomplish his will within his "domain" or within himself. According to the second interpretation, "heaven" refers to the cosmos inaccessible to man. "Earth" is what is given to him for his "domination." The familiar biblical expression "heaven and earth," then, designates creation in its entirety.

All creation is the language of divine will: "And God said, 'Let there be light'; and there was light" (Genesis 1:3). It expresses something of the beauty of God because it is an act of God the Creator. "I questioned the sky, the sun, the moon and the stars. They declared to me, 'We are not God, it is he who made us.'" That is the way Augustine, in his *Confessions* (X:9), explained the divine splendor and coherence of creation.

God created "earth" as a dwelling place for the men and women to whom he communicates his holy will through the commandments of the Covenant. God's order is one of law and the redemption of mankind.

"Thy will be done on earth as it is in heaven" translates as "Accomplish your will, O God, in the hearts of your children so that they will desire to love and serve you, and in so doing will be singing your glory, already so magnificently proclaimed by all creation."

* * *

The same parallel between God's creation of the heavens and his law intended for man can be found in Psalm 19, which consists of two parts linked together by the Psalmist in an inseparable fashion.

By his word, God created the heavens which fulfill his plan of creation:

> The heavens are telling the glory
>   of God;
>   and the firmament proclaims
>   his handiwork.
> Day to day pours forth speech,
>   and night to night declares
>   knowledge.
> There is no speech, nor are there
>   words;
>   their voice is not heard;

yet their voice goes through all the
    earth,
and their words to the end of the
    world. . . .
             — Psalm 19:1-4

By his word, God has also given
his law to man so that the divine will
can be accomplished on earth:
The law of the LORD is perfect,
    reviving the soul;
the testimony of the LORD is sure,
    making wise the simple;
the precepts of the LORD are right,
    rejoicing the heart;
the commandment of the LORD is
    pure,
    enlightening the eyes;
. . .
    O LORD, my rock and my
    redeemer.
             — Psalm 19:7-8, 14

Thus, Psalm 19, made up of two
distinct parts that interlock and
complement each other, gives thanks

for the will of God which has been "done," that is, accomplished "on earth as in heaven."

* * *

When we pray, "Father, thy will be done on earth as it is in heaven. . ." — in other words, "accomplish your will in me and in all your children" — we are participating in the creative act of God because we are embracing his redemptive plan for all the world.

"Thy will be done." Praying these words when facing difficulties or misfortune does not imply resigning ourselves to the inescapable. On the contrary, completely free, we enter into God's plan: asking him — *in spite of the circumstances* — to accomplish *in* us and *for* us what he wants us to do.

Finally, the expression "on earth as it is in heaven" is a reminder that each instant of our lives takes its singular place in the universal chorus which sings the splendor of God.

« 12 »

'My food is to do the will of him who sent me'

Do you recall Job's prayer when he was in the throes of the mystery of evil? Struggling to keep from being crushed, with his faith being tested in the extreme, he cried, ". . . the LORD gave, and the LORD has taken away; blessed be the name of the LORD" (Job 1:21). But when we pray, ". . . thy will be done," we are not, like Job, submitting to a fatality with blind resignation. We are praying that we shall be able with all our being to conform to the will of God, that we can *live* the will of God.

We are meant to react like Jesus who says, "My food is to do the will of him who sent me" (John 4:34). But in order to recognize that the will of the Father is our food, it is necessary to *desire* to do his will.

* * *

Jesus tells us this when, during the Feast of the Tabernacles, he is teaching in the temple: "If any man's will is to do his [that is, God's] will, he shall know whether the teaching is from God or whether I am speaking on my own authority" (John 7:17). Whoever communes with the will of God recognizes the will of God. He is, as the saying goes, "on the same wavelength." And if there is "static" between God and man, it is the sin of man which is at fault.

Remember, too, the remark of the blind man after healing, ". . . if any one is a worshiper of God and does his will, God listens to him" (John 9:31). And, at the resurrection of Lazarus, Jesus prays aloud to his Father, "I knew that thou hearest me always, but I have said this on account of the people standing by, that they may believe that thou didst send me" (John 11:42).

I would venture to say that whoever does the will of God has his will done by God. This audacious truth was taught by Jesus at his last Passover: "If you abide in me, and my words abide in you, ask whatever you will, and it shall be done for you" (John 15:7). Far from being fatalistic, praying "thy will be done" let us receive from God the strength to be heard in our prayer. What an unexpected perspective Christ opens to us here!

* * *

Christ says that we "ought always to pray and not lose heart" (Luke 18:1).

He gives us the example of the widow who, through the tenacity of her supplications, obliges the judge "who neither feared God nor regarded men" to "vindicate her." He concludes

the parable by reversing the idea that
we have of God since he presents us
with an unrighteous and heartless
judge — as if God were deaf and silent.
He then adds, "And will not God
vindicate his elect, who cry to him day
and night? Will he delay long over
them? I tell you, he will vindicate them
speedily. Nevertheless, when the Son
of man comes, will he find faith on
earth?" (Luke 18:7-8).

The first three requests of the
"Lord's Prayer" might be summed up
as "asking God to vindicate us":

> We ask that his name be hallowed,
> and that his kingdom of justice
>> come
> through the accomplishment of
>> his will;
> that is, we ask him to permit us
> to have a part in his plan of
>> salvation.

* * *

Jesus' part in God's plan of
salvation entails his Passion. Just
prior to telling the parable about the

judge who was so persistently importuned by the widow, Jesus states that before the coming of the kingdom of God "the Son of man . . . first . . . must suffer many things and be rejected by this generation" (Luke 17:24-25). The disciples will understand what he is saying only *after* the resurrection when Jesus will have given them the Holy Spirit and opened their hearts to the mystery of the cross. Remember how he asks the men on the road to Emmaus, "Was it not necessary that the Christ should suffer these things and enter into his glory?" (Luke 24:26).

When Jesus prays, "Father . . . thy will be done," he is expressing his fervent desire for the realization of God's plan of salvation for his people and all humanity. It is that desire which nourishes his prayer in all the circumstances of his life, whether he is weeping over the death of Lazarus or over the city he loves: "O Jerusalem, Jerusalem, killing the prophets and stoning those who are sent to you! How often would I have gathered your children together as a hen gathers her brood under her wings, and you would not!" (Luke 13:34).

When we pray, "Father . . . thy will be done," we are expressing *our* desire to take part, along with Christ, Savior of men, in God's plan.

« 13 »

Your place in God's plan

The "Lord's Prayer" is not to be prayed with resignation: "Father, what will happen will happen," or "Since it's an order, I'll obey" — as though we were being called to attention by a spiritual commander in chief. Such an attitude would indicate that "the servant does not know what his master is doing" (John 15:15), which is not at all the case. He who has given up his life guides us along his path, making us acquainted with God's will so that we do it freely. And the will of God is that each of us contributes to the salvation of mankind. Once we know this, a prodigious perspective opens up before us, affecting both our prayers and daily existence.

The dimension of that perspective was beautifully articulated by Paul when he wrote to the Christians at Philippia: "For me to live is Christ and to die is gain. If it is to be life in the flesh, that means fruitful labor for me. Yet which I shall choose I cannot tell. I am hard pressed between the two. My desire is to depart and be with Christ, for that is far better. But to remain in the flesh is more necessary on your account. Convinced of this, I know that I shall remain and continue with you all, for your progress and joy in the faith, so that in me you may have ample cause to glory in Christ Jesus, because of my coming to you again" (1:21-26). The Apostle to the "pagan nations" is keenly aware that his life is inscribed in the universal plan for salvation.

And what about our lives?

Whether afflicted or relatively carefree, we are tempted to focus on ourselves in our dialogue with God. So be it. "My Creator and myself," as Cardinal Newman used to say. It is, of course, true that our singular one-to-one relationship with God is the foundation of our faith. But "my" Creator is also the Creator of "all my brothers and sisters." Each one of us is included in God's universal plan, and our respective lives are projected into the context of God's love for all humanity.

You who are elderly and exhausted may be saying to yourselves, "I'm ready now to go on and be with God." You who suffer, who have been abandoned, who weep, may be questioning, "Why should I go on living? There's no one around to listen to me, no one for whom my existence matters." But it is precisely *you* who, by your interior offering, must carry everyone else in your prayers. Unite yourself to Christ, who says with your

lips, "Thy will be done." You share in
the power of Christ's intercession. You
must struggle until the end and offer
what you are enduring, not only for
those whom you know, but for the
entire Church and all the world.

Every instant of every life counts
in the history of humanity's salvation.

* * *

I can suggest some verses from the
Psalms which will help you to enlarge
your heart in order to pray with
Christ, "Our Father . . . thy will be
done on earth as it is in heaven":

Then I said, "Lo, I come;
in the roll of the book it is
written of me;
I delight to do thy will, O my God;
thy law is within my heart."
I have told the glad news of
deliverance
in the great congregation;
lo, I have not restrained my lips,
as thou knowest, O LORD.
— Psalm 40:7-9

O LORD, thou hast searched me
and known me!
Thou knowest when I sit down and
when I rise up;
thou discernest my thoughts
from afar.
. . .
Thy eyes beheld my unformed
substance;
in thy book were written, every
one of them,
the days that were formed for me,
when as yet there was none of
them.
— Psalm 139:1-2, 16

Praying "thy will be done" must
be understood not as an acceptance of
fate, but as an acknowledgment of our
vocation.

God calls you to work with Christ
in the laborious construction of your
life which cannot be reduced to
professional accomplishments. Neither
can the fruits of your existence be
weighed by the number of children

brought up, students taught, or objects produced. Nothing of this nature suffices for an "accounting" because *everything* in your life counts — but only as it relates to God.

You cannot possibly know the worth of your life. It is determined by the extent to which the Spirit permits you, along with Christ in the Church, to carry out God's will for you, what he wants you to do for the world's salvation.

* * *

In summary, then, we ask in the first three requests of the "Lord's Prayer" that God accomplish what he wills, that is, that he be God.

In the second part of the prayer, "we" appear. At this point, we pray as pilgrims whom Christ is leading through the desert in a new exodus, as God's people whom Christ is calling to follow him toward the eternal Passover.

« 14 »

'Give us this day our daily bread'

The first phrases of the "Lord's Prayer" orient us toward God's plan for the world's salvation: we ask God to act according to his will and promise. The words we pray, however, will have no meaning for us unless we commit ourselves to becoming similar to the only Son, and pray them in the spirit that he prayed them: the desire for the coming of God's kingdom pervades every moment of Christ's life.

For most of us, time passes either much too quickly — when we are absorbed in some interesting or amusing activity; or much too slowly — when we are bored or doing "chores." The result is that we are frequently "absent" from the *present instant* in which our lives are being inscribed in the history of salvation.

For Christ, on the contrary, every instant as well as every event of his life contributes to the coming of the kingdom. Entirely free, he recuperates each fragment of his existence and makes a total offering of himself to the Father so that his "will be done." In teaching us to pray, Christ is simultaneously teaching us how to *live as he lives*: for the Son of God-made-man, all sin calls for forgiveness; all misery, for healing; all distress, for God's salvation. Furthermore, he shows us that every moment of our existence is an occasion for thanksgiving, a time for our hearts to sing the glory of God.

As we pray the first three requests of the "Lord's Prayer" — in Christ, by the power of the Holy Spirit

— we are uniting ourselves with what God is and does; we are praying that he will accomplish what he wants to accomplish. We are thereby engaging ourselves in the "work" of God, Creator and Savior of the world. It becomes our "business." And our business is God's business:

". . . hallowed be thy name. Thy kingdom come, thy will be done. . . ."

* * *

In the second part of the prayer, the perspective seems to be reversed: it focuses on us. Note that the personal pronoun is used six times: "Give *us* this day . . . forgive *us* our trespasses, as *we* forgive those who trespass against *us* . . . lead *us* not . . . but deliver *us* from evil."

"Give us this day our daily bread."

Initially, such a request can seem strange — not only because for some people bread is no longer a vital and desirable form of nourishment but also because we all know that the vast majority of people have to *earn* their bread by hard work.

Are we then petitioning God for a kind of "living allowance"? Would that not imply that we were irresponsible, incapable of providing for our needs? Would it not contradict the precept of God himself, given at the dawn of humanity: "In the sweat of your face you shall eat your bread" (Genesis 3:19), and also Paul's exhortation to the people of Thessalonica: ". . . work with your hands, as we charged you" (1 Thessalonians 4:11)?

No, the request is not an appeal to be exempted from labor; however, an explanation is needed. In the phrase "Give us this day our daily bread," the words "this day" have influenced the translators' choice of nuance regarding the adjective preceding "bread." The word "daily" masks the complexity of the Greek word which has a "four-sided" meaning: "Supersubstantial, necessary, tomorrow's, daily." These meanings form a whole precisely as patches of color do in an impressionist painting. More or less connected, when taken together they convey the full richness which the Aramaic expression had as Christ himself spoke it.

It is edifying to consider these aspects of the Aramaic expression as they refer to Christ's teachings, being careful to keep in mind their accumulated meaning as we pass from one to the other.

* * *

The complex Greek word chosen for Christ's expression was subsequently translated by early Christians into Latin as "quotidianus" from which both the French and English words — "quotidien," "quotidian" — are derived.

Jesus places a great deal of emphasis on living from day to day. He says, for example, in the Sermon on the Mount, "Therefore do not be anxious, saying, 'What shall we eat?' or 'What shall we drink?' or 'What shall we wear?' . . . your heavenly Father

knows that you need them all. . . . Do
not be anxious about tomorrow, for
tomorrow will be anxious for itself. Let
the day's own trouble be sufficient for
the day" (Matthew 6:31-34).

* * *

"What man of you, if his son asks
him for bread, will give him a stone?"
(Matthew 7:9).

By having us ask the Father in
heaven for daily bread, Jesus is calling
on us to have confidence in the Father,
to begin each day by placing anew our
lives in his hands.

Such was the case with God's
people who, during their ordeal in the
desert, gathered only one day's portion
of manna at a time, having been
forbidden to make provisions for the
following day — except for the
Sabbath (cf. Exodus 16:4ff.). We must
learn, like them, to receive all, every
day — *today* — from God and God
alone.

Asking for "daily" bread,
entrusting their lives to God from day

to day was the formative experience of Israel: wandering in the desert, dispossessed of everything, they receive the greatest of riches, that of being constituted as God's people. Israel becomes itself, thanks to God who gives of himself in the mystery of the Covenant. God is their life and he nourishes them. In return, they are asked to have faith, which means recognizing God who recognizes every human being and sustains his existence.

* * *

We are also asking God to give us the bread we need as we travel along the earthly road to the heavenly kingdom: the Eucharist.

Christ multiplies bread for the hungry crowds who have been nourished by his word. By the power of the word of God, he performs a miracle which renews the marvel of manna, "the bread of the strong," the "bread of the angels" (Psalm 78:25). But, at the same time, his miracle is the prophecy of our Christian condition in the era of the Church when the eucharistic bread nourishes and unites the messianic people — Christ's brothers and sisters journeying toward the kingdom of heaven.

* * *

This facet of the translation brings to mind the banquet of the heavenly kingdom at the end of time, the feast prophesied by Isaiah: "On this mountain the LORD of hosts will make for all peoples a feast. . . . It will be said on that day, 'Lo, this is our God' " (25:6ff.).

Jesus announces this banquet when he institutes the Eucharist: "I tell you I shall not drink again of this fruit of the vine until that day when I drink it new with you in my Father's kingdom" (Matthew 26:29).

In the Book of Joshua, it is related that after Israel's first harvest in Canaan ". . . the manna ceased on the morrow, when they ate of the produce of the land; and the people of Israel had manna no more, but ate of the fruit of the land of Canaan that year" (5:12). The bread "for tomorrow" refers to the first bread of the Promised Land. Jesus, "the bread of life, who comes down from heaven" (cf. John 6:32-35), instructs us to ask God to let us partake of the banquet which will take place in the Promised Land, the land of eternal life.

"Give us this day our daily bread": "Give us the manna for today which will permit us to continue our journey toward the Promised Land, the heavenly kingdom." Although that kingdom will be revealed in its full splendor only at the end of time, we nevertheless ask God to let us taste — today — the ultimate bread of the eternal banquet. The Eucharist is both the bread for travelers *toward* the kingdom and the bread *of* the kingdom. It is Christ giving of himself as the nourishment of eternal life.

The "Lord's Prayer" has us ask for the nourishment intended for the people of the new exodus, God's people for whom *he* is the source of life. We are led, through Christ, to receive all from God at every instant, and to give back our lives to him.

* * *

Exactly how does Jesus pray for his "daily bread"?

• When he is tempted in the desert, Jesus' prayer is a great ordeal. He foresees what he will have to ask for, because after fasting for forty days, "he was hungry." But he resists temptation and gives himself life by using the divine power received in his humanity from his Father. He answers the Tempter, "It is written, 'Man shall not live by bread alone, but by every word that proceeds from the mouth of God' " (Matthew 4:4; see also Deuteronomy 8:3). Jesus receives his nourishment from God alone, thus accomplishing the will of God perfectly. For Jesus, asking God for "bread" is not simply a solicitation of a vital minimum, just enough to sustain him; he is also asking for the "bread of life" with an attitude of total availability to the Father from whom all life comes. "Do not lay up for yourselves treasures on earth, where moth and rust consume and where thieves break in and steal, but lay up for yourselves treasures in heaven, where neither moth nor rust consumes and where thieves do not break in and steal. For where your treasure is, there will your heart be also" (Matthew 6:19-21).

• When multiplying bread to feed the hungry crowd, Jesus "looked up to heaven, and blessed, and broke and gave the loaves to the disciples, and the disciples gave them to the crowds" (Matthew 14:19; see also Mark 6:41; Luke 9:16).

• Finally, when Jesus prays at the Last Supper, ". . . he took bread, and when he had given thanks he broke it and gave it to them, saying, 'This is my body which is given for you. Do this in remembrance of me' " (Luke 22:19).

« 15 »

'You do not know what you are asking'

By instructing us to ask God to "give us this day our daily bread," Jesus underlines the rapport between the events of our daily existence — including our worries about tomorrow — and the attitude inherent in his prayer: one of complete trust in God.

In order to teach us the omnipotence of his confident prayer to our Father in heaven, Jesus poses a question: ". . . what man of you, if his son asks for bread, will give him a stone?" (Matthew 6:9). At first, the image surprises. But it derives from

Jesus' prayer after forty days of fasting in the desert, when the devil tempts him to change the "stones to become loaves of bread."

The evangelists make a point of showing us just how much Jesus "premeditated," desired, and anticipated by his prayer in the desert the multiplication of bread and his last Passover celebration, where God gives "daily bread." Thus, from the beginning of his ministry, Jesus prays with his regard and his heart already turned toward his imminent Passion and the offering of his life that he is going to make to the Father. "I have a baptism to be baptized with; and how I am constrained until it is accomplished!" (Luke 12:50). These words direct us again to the ultimate prayer of his Passion.

In fact, saying to God, "Give us this day our daily bread," is tantamount to saying, "I want to receive the life that comes from 'everything that proceeds out of the mouth of the LORD' (Deuteronomy 8:3)." It also joins us to the prayer of the crucified Christ from Psalm 31, reiterated in the Gospel of Luke: "Father, into thy hands I commit my spirit!" (23:46).

"I have earnestly desired to eat *this* passover with you before I suffer," Jesus confides to his apostles (Luke 22:15 — emphasis author's). He wishes specifically to be able to share with them the traditional Passover prayer which he enlarges to encompass the feast of "the last day": "for I tell you I shall not eat it until it is fulfilled in the kingdom of God" (Luke 22:16).

* * *

We must allow the rich harmonies of the "Lord's Prayer" to reverberate in us, over and over again.

"Give us this day our daily bread" can also refer to certain events foreseen for the coming day: an important decision to be made, a person to be met; in short, all the activities that we expect to take part in.

Nevertheless, when I ask God to give me his light for making a certain decision, his strength for a particular project to be undertaken, his love for a difficult personal encounter, I leave — with an attitude of filial abandon — the granting of my requests to God's discretion.

Furthermore, when united with Christ I ask for "daily bread" (*epiousion*, transliteration of the Greek for "supersubstantial"), my prayer is joined to the sacrament of the Eucharist. Not only because "on this day" I am participating in the Eucharist, but also because the Word of God-made-flesh is being given to me as nourishment and transforms me into what I receive: the body of Christ.

The future, however, will always remain undetermined, beyond our control. Asking God to "give us our daily bread — for *tomorrow*" implies trusting him to the point that, in a manner of speaking, we are giving him a blank check for our future. Because when we make spontaneous and specific requests — for today, for tomorrow — we should keep in mind Jesus' response to the sons of Zebedee who wanted to sit beside him in his glory: "You do not know what you are asking" (Mark 10:38). In praying the "Lord's Prayer," I accept then to trust in God to give me the "daily bread" to face all the unexpected things which can happen in my life: happiness or misfortune, sickness or health, length or brevity of my days on earth, solitude or communion. I do this with the utmost assurance because "God is faithful, by whom you were called into the fellowship of his Son, Jesus Christ our Lord. . . . [He] will sustain you to the end, guiltless in the day of our Lord Jesus Christ" (1 Corinthians 1:9 and 1:8).

When this request is made realistically, in the context of our daily lives we orient ourselves to the ultimate coming of the kingdom of God and the glorious return of Christ whom we love "without having seen him" (1 Peter 1:8). As Paul affirms, ". . . now we see in a mirror dimly, but then face to face. Now I know in part; then I shall understand fully, even as I have been fully understood" (1 Corinthians 13:12). And he continues, "When all things are subjected to him, then the Son himself will also be subjected to him who put all things under him, that God may be everything to every one" (1 Corinthians 15:28).

"My God, be my nourishment each day of my life until I reach the eternal Passover that I so much long for."

#《 16 》

'Forgive us our trespasses. . .'

In the opening sentences of the "Lord's Prayer," we ask for the accomplishment of the will of God, that is, the coming of his kingdom. The second part of the prayer reflects the needs of a people, marching along with Christ in the new exodus, who wish to be instruments of that accomplishment. First, we ask for life, heavenly manna; and immediately afterward, we ask for forgiveness.

Why does the request for forgiveness come at such a central point? Because there is an intimate connection between forgiveness (received from God and given to our brothers and sisters) and prayer.

Keep in mind the admonition of Jesus: "And whenever you stand praying, forgive, if you have anything against any one; so that your Father also who is in heaven may forgive your trespasses" (Mark 11:25).

In the Gospel of Matthew, we find these words of Jesus, "For if you forgive men their trespasses, your heavenly Father also will forgive you; but if you do not forgive men their trespasses, neither will your Father forgive your trespasses" (6:14-15).

Accordingly, when Jesus teaches the disciples "his prayer" — after his instruction on giving alms and before his remarks on fasting — he develops only one of the requests. And that request is at the very heart of his teaching on prayer: *forgive*.

Forgiveness and faith

When Jesus stresses the connection between forgiving and

praying — "so that your Father also who is in heaven may forgive your trespasses" (Mark 11:25) — he has just taught the lesson of the unfruitful fig tree, cursed by him and completely withered from one day to the next. The people of God have been given the law so that they will bear the fruits of holiness; the fig tree symbolizes the person who bears no fruit and is thus considered dead. How do we become capable of acting according to the divine will? How can we be saved? Not surprisingly, the disciples are frightened by the stringent demands of the kingdom. Peter, however, understands intuitively this prophetic gesture of the Lord who explains, "Have faith in God."

"Having faith in God" is neither the self-persuasion of a fanatic who declares, "I'm right! Everyone else is wrong!"; nor is it the firm conviction that we can ask God for anything at all. "Having faith" means depending on God's strength alone. To live the faith is to be sure of God, even when we are no longer sure of ourselves; to have no doubts about God's power even when we have doubts about our own strength; to count on God and not on the short-term evidence of our experience.

God gives us the strength to accomplish what he asks us to do; what he requires he permits us to do; what he promises he expects from us.

Therefore, the forgiveness which God commands, and which seems impossible to us, is made possible by him.

Forgiveness and the Passion

Christian forgiveness can take place only when a person has complete faith in God, as is illustrated by Mark's description of Jesus during his Passion.

Forgiveness is not resigned indulgence bordering on cowardliness; not a complacent forgetting or a searching for excuses; not an indifference to the pain of an offense. But neither is it compatible with holding a grudge or hating. And that may seem virtually impossible when our emotions have been subjected to overwhelmingly intense suffering.

The ability to forgive, for which we ask in our prayer, is a deep mystery. It tests our relationship with God just as fire tests gold in a crucible. It places us at the heart of the paschal mystery.

Forgiveness, in fact, is the hallmark of Jesus' prayer on the cross: "Father, forgive them; for they know not what they do" (Luke 23:34). He does not excuse them; he *forgives* them in praying to the Father to forgive them. He offers his life to the Father for the salvation of all humanity, his brothers and his sisters.

((17))

Jesus gives the Father's pardon to humanity

John the Baptist preached and gave "a baptism of repentance for the forgiveness of sins" (Luke 3:3). Christ not only placed forgiveness at the heart of his preaching, but he comes to the world for its accomplishment. He paid for it with his blood in the sacrifice of the New Covenant (cf. Luke 22:20).

The power to forgive sins which Jesus entrusts to the apostles (cf. Luke 24:47; John 20:23) is given to him by his Father as he clearly reveals:

- When he heals the paralytic

man at Capernaum (cf. Mark 2:1-12;
Luke 5:17-26; Matthew 9:1-8), and says,
"My son, your sins are forgiven," the
implication is: "God has forgiven your
sins." Jesus acts as only God can act. It
is not surprising that the scribes and
Pharisees are astonished. Jesus
responds, "Why do you question thus
in your hearts? Which is easier, to say
to the paralytic, 'Your sins are
forgiven,' or to say, 'Rise, take up your
pallet and walk'?" (Mark 2:8-9). Jesus
heals the paralytic so that he "may
know that the Son of man has
authority on earth to forgive sins"
(Mark 2:10).

• There is the woman sinner who,
during Jesus' dinner at Simon's house,
wets his feet with her tears (Luke
7:36-50). Simon is scandalized because
he is unaware of what God has done
for her. Jesus, however, knows that his
Father has pardoned her, and she, who
was a sinner, knows that Jesus brings
the forgiveness of the Father; hence,
her gestures — incomprehensible to

others — of gratitude and love for her Redeemer and Savior.

Jesus forgives sins in the name of the Father. Through the work of redemption, the Son becomes the instrument of God's forgiveness.

* * *

By teaching us to pray, ". . . as we forgive those who trespass against us," Jesus is taking the teaching of the rabbis and giving it a depth all the more extraordinary because he is himself both the victim and the priest by whom God accomplishes the definitive remission of sins. He, Christ, is "the Lamb of God, who takes away the sin of the world!" (John 1:29). He "did this once and for all when he offered up himself" and "he is able for all time to save those who draw near to God through him, since he always lives to make intercession for them." (See Hebrews 7:21-27.) The people of Israel understood very well, and Christian doctrine has always taught, that for faults committed toward a neighbor, forgiveness must be obtained not only from God but also from the offended brother or sister. The wrong must be repaired and there must be reconciliation with the hope of obtaining the forgiveness which is the victim's duty to give. There is also an important corollary to this teaching, regarding the number of times we are to forgive someone who sins against us. When Peter poses the question, Jesus replies, ". . . seventy times seven" (Matthew 18:22). His answer is a reminder of a passage from Genesis: "If Cain is avenged sevenfold, truly Lamech seventy-seven fold" (4:24). In this instance, God, always just, must assure that the murderer of an innocent person atones for his act. But the requirements for fraternal forgiveness go far beyond justice. This being so, how could we possibly imagine that we would be able to pardon if we relied on our own strength alone?

Remember the commentary that

Jesus made on the commandment of God, "You have heard that it was said to the men of old, 'You shall not kill; and whoever kills shall be liable to judgment.' But I say to you that every one who is angry with his brother shall be liable to judgment; whoever insults his brother shall be liable to council, and whoever says, 'You fool!' shall be liable to the hell of fire. So if you are offering your gift at the altar, and there remember that your brother has something against you, leave your gift there before the altar and go; first be reconciled to your brother, and then come and offer your gift" (Matthew 5:21-24). Jesus goes even further regarding the duty of forgiveness connected to the offering of a sacrifice and inscribes it in the very impulse of prayer.

What kind of forgiveness do we ask of God? Not a forgetting, as if nothing has ever happened; that makes no sense. Not an amnesty, nor a statute of limitation. No! God's forgiveness differs from all judicial forms of pardon. The punishment for our faults belongs to the mystery of God who, on Judgment Day, will lead us to discover our lives in the light of his truth.

Asking God to forgive us means asking him to *re-create* us, because sin is the destruction of ourselves. "O God, make us a part of your new creation. O God, create in us pure hearts."

Is it possible then for us to forgive our brothers and sisters in the way that God forgives us? Is it the *same* kind of forgiveness? Yes, because forgiveness is at the heart of redemption which gives us life and makes it possible for us to give life to others.

« 18 »

Forgive, as a forgiven sinner

"I cannot pray the 'Lord's Prayer' to the end because I cannot bring myself to forgive." Have you ever felt that way? How is it possible for someone with such feelings to go ahead and pray — without being dishonest — the words that Jesus puts on our lips: "Forgive us . . . as we forgive. . ."?

If the forgiveness that Christ commands us to grant our debtors is so difficult for us, it is because it requires us to act toward them as God himself acts toward us, that is, divinely, with the power of God.

In other words, God's forgiveness must *dwell within us*. But that may seem hopeless, unless it is for our own forgiveness that we are appealing. However, Christ is constantly interceding for us; he is the "great high priest," as the Letter to the Hebrews (4:14) points out. But at what a cost! Jesus does not distribute the Father's forgiveness cautiously, like a nuclear engineer who must protect himself from the source of the energy he works with. No! Christ gives us the forgiveness of the Father by fulfilling the act of redemption, by giving of himself unstintingly, all the way to the mystery of the cross. Why are you surprised, then, that it is so very difficult to forgive? *Forgiveness is always crucifying.*

* * *

In order to forgive one another, we must enter into the mystery of the cross; we are sinners who have ourselves been forgiven, thanks to the sacrament of reconciliation.

So, the first step toward forgiving is to go, in a sincere gesture of humility, and ask God to forgive you. Confess your resistance to the act of forgiving, acknowledge your unwillingness to follow Christ in his Passion. Once you do, God will give you, as a grace, the capacity required to fulfill your mission which is to forgive, in union with Christ crucified and resurrected.

In the sacrament of reconciliation, Christ takes our hearts of stone in his hands and transforms them into hearts of flesh. Only then does a heart discover how little it has loved God who loves it unconditionally. We can again become sensitive to the love given to us by Christ, the one who restores life to those who seem dead, like the daughter of Jairus (Mark 5:35). Resentments, harshness, the inability to pardon — all of these will disappear as we are pardoned for these faults by Christ. When, in the sacrament of penance, or reconciliation, we ask Christ to heal us, we are already beginning to forgive. We must partake of the mystery of the cross as forgiven sinners, as though we were one of the criminals hanged with Christ — the one who rebuked the other for railing at Christ to save them. Do you remember his words? " 'Do you not fear God, since you are under the same sentence of condemnation? And we indeed justly; for we are receiving the due reward of our deeds; but this man has done nothing wrong.' And he said, 'Jesus, remember me when you come in your kingly power.' And he said to him, 'Truly, I say to you, today you will be with me in Paradise' " (Luke 23:40-43). Having acknowledged ourselves as sinners, we are then privileged to participate in the redeeming act of Christ.

* * *

There are several steps which you can take in order to give yourself the strength to forgive.

First of all, during the celebration of the Eucharist, enter into these parts of the liturgy with all your heart.

• The penitential rite at the beginning of the Mass will allow you to recall and repent of your sins in silence. Pray, "Lord, give me the gift of a contrite heart."

• In the grace of your own forgiveness springing from Christ's sacrifice, share the sign of the peace of Christ with your brothers and sisters before you partake of our Lord's body. Because God has forgiven us, we can forgive one another.

Present yourself before God as a pauper. Begin by making some modest but concrete gestures which will be seen only by your heavenly Father:

• Fast. (This is not to be confused with going on a hunger strike!) Make a concerted effort to overcome the defenses of your body (because, as you know very well, the incapacity to forgive is also inscribed in the biological condition of our existence), and let yourself be sustained by God. Make yourself weak, stripping yourself of personal strength so that God can act.

• Give alms. By using money as an instrument of love, deprive yourself of a means of power and thus, possibly, of a means of vengeance which money can become. Deny some of your own needs and give the money to those who are less fortunate.

• Meditate on Christ's Passion. Using either the gospel accounts or the Stations of the Cross in a church, follow our Lord from Gethsemane to Calvary.

• Pray Psalms of penitence (in particular Psalms 30, 31, 32, 51, and 130). Pray them with the awareness that you are united with Christ and all the sinners of the world.

When we pray, ". . . and forgive us our trespasses, as we forgive those who trespass against us," we are asking God to make it possible for us to forgive as Christ forgave. It goes without saying that such a request obliges us like Christ to rely on *God's* strength, and, hence, to receive it as a grace and a gift.

((19))

'Lead us not into temptation'

Although the expression "lead us
not into temptation" comes close to the
Greek from which it was translated, it
does not convey the precise sense of the
Aramaic in which Jesus spoke the
words. It can understandably
disconcert us since it is impossible to
imagine that God would "lead into
evil" the people whom he loves and
calls to a life of holiness.

The strong arguments put forth
by biblical exegetists for modifying the
translation have not yet succeeded, but
we must interpret the meaning as it is
understood by these scholars: "Father,

keep us from entering into temptation."

* * *

In modern usage, the word "temptation" as presented by the advertising world connotes an impulsive desire to which it is pleasant to succumb even if doing so may be rather imprudent — for example, breaking a diet or allowing yourself a lapse in the way you usually spend your money.

In moral life, temptation is the attraction of forbidden fruit and tests our faithfulness to a law. Whether the pleasure comes from the fruit or the fact that it is forbidden is a question that can be left to psychologists. But it is classic for moral choices to be represented in a Herculean manner, with a person hesitating between the paths of sin and of virtue. And yet, good and evil cannot have a comparable attraction. Man can be tempted by evil only when it *appears* to promise a certain good. Thus, in moral life desirable goods must be rationally weighed and rated.

Human reactions to temptation can also be arranged in ascending order, from the most instinctive — that is, reducible to biological reactions — to the most reasonable. A conscience which has complete mastery over blind desires copes with them sensibly; indeed, it sublimates them. In that case, yielding to temptation would consist of ceding to our "animality" to the detriment of our "humanity," of ceding to our instinctive drives or physical desires to the detriment of our reason.

In such conflicts, we confront *ourselves*.

* * *

In the Bible, the spiritual experience of temptation is altogether different. Here, temptation is a kind of struggle which puts man's relationship to God to the test.

Jacob underwent such a temptation in his nightlong combat with the angel on the edge of the ford of the Jabbok. Rather than struggling with himself, Jacob, in order to triumph, must consent to God who, he senses, is behind the mysterious combatant. And God, in a way, must in turn submit himself to Jacob, his creature in whom he wishes to dwell. "When the man saw that he did not prevail against Jacob, he touched the hollow of his thigh; . . . Then he said, 'Your name shall no more be called Jacob, but Israel, for you have striven with God and with men, and have prevailed.' " (See Genesis 32:22-33.) This astonishing story sketches the apparent contradictions in the mystical experience which is the loving relationship between God and humanity.

For Jacob, temptation is the test of his fidelity to the "jealous" love of God. Man is tempted to refuse to love

God by replacing him with an idol
fashioned by his own desires. And that
comes down to man's loving himself to
the point of despising God. Thus, he
cuts himself off from God, the source
of all life and all love. In this
perspective, we can understand that
God's "jealousy" is his grief at seeing
men and women wounded by their own
unfaithfulness.

* * *

In the background of this spiritual
temptation which is the choice
between two loves — love of self or
love of God — emerges the figure of
the Tempter, Satan, "the father of lies"
(John 8:44), the blasphemer, the denial
of God, and the power of darkness who
seeks to make man his accomplice.

It is, then, a choice between these
two loves which is the supreme ordeal
of spiritual combat where sin and
redemption are mixed. In this agony at
Gethsemane, Christ vanquishes this
temptation for us by enduring his

Passion. Therefore, it is in the spiritual choice (for or against God) that the moral choice (for or against good) discovers the true stakes around which temptation revolves.

« 20 »

'Satan demanded to have you . . . but I have prayed. . .'

Already in apostolic times, some
Greek-speaking Christians
misinterpreted the expression "lead us
not into temptation" as meaning that
temptation comes from God. James
vigorously corrects their error in his
letter: "Let no one say when he is
tempted, 'I am tempted by God'; for
God cannot be tempted with evil and
he himself tempts no one; but each
person is tempted when he is lured and
enticed by his own desire" (1:13-14). If
this were not true, God would be

nothing more than the projection of man's heart, and serving him would be the worst of slaveries. But, "thanks be to God," it is we who are created in *his* image. . . .

God does not "lead us into temptation," but *temptation* leads us into a spiritual combat which forces us to make a choice: are we for or against God? This is where the real choice lies, where the real struggle takes place. Conceiving of moral life as separate from our relationship to God is an illusion of our technological civilization which reduces the body, the senses, and even reason to objects to be manipulated. The Bible, however, makes it clear: *nothing* which touches man is extraneous as far as God is concerned. Whether a person acknowledges it or not, his moral life and attitude toward God are inscribed in the very condition of his having been created in God's image. Fundamentally, then, temptation turns around this relationship between the Creator and his creature.

* * *

"Lead us not into temptation" should be interpreted as meaning "Keep us from entering into temptation." Among the many biblical references to temptation, there are two which are particularly significant. The first one is found at the beginning of Genesis: "So God created man in his own image, in the image of God he created him; male and female he created them" (1:27); "Now the serpent was more subtle than any other wild creature that the LORD God had made" (3:1).

The original temptation illustrates the nature of *all* temptation. The vocation of man, who is made in the image of God, destines him for the happiness which derives from his communion with the divine will. By cutting himself off from the source of life, by turning away from his Creator and Father, man deprives himself of life because he has chosen sin and death instead.

The second reference, found near the end of the Book of Exodus, relates the temptation of the chosen people while they were still in the desert: "When the people saw that Moses delayed to come down from the mountains, the people gathered themselves together to Aaron, and said to him, 'Up, make us gods, who shall go before us; as for this Moses, the man who brought us up out of the land of Egypt, we do not know what has become of him' " (32:1).

God gives his law to the people of Israel, and they thus receive the bounty of his life. Called to be holy, they are henceforth able to live as his children, created in his image and resemblance. But fear may cause them to turn their backs on God and to make gods, such as the golden calf, in their own resemblance and manner.

* * *

What connection is there between man's temptations and the temptations of Christ?

Sinful man, in his wounded state, is blind to his true destiny. A prisoner of his drives, he does not realize against what and against whom he is fighting when he is tempted. He is fascinated by diverse desires (sensual pleasures, power, money, revenge), and he sees nothing else.

Christ, "who knew no sin," was "made . . . to be sin" (2 Corinthians 5:21), and entered into the spiritual combat of sinful man. He emerged victorious in the mystery of his Passion. It is, in fact, *our* temptations which become his ordeal since he bears them on his shoulders. But he, unlike unseeing man, clearly sees his adversary, Satan, who "prowls around like a roaring lion, seeking some one to devour" (1 Peter 5:8). Furthermore, he unveils the stakes of the battle: whether we shall adore God and him alone, or whether we shall become prisoners of his Enemy who "was a murderer from the beginning, and has nothing to do with the truth, because there is no truth in him" (John 8:44). The only way that we can expose the devil, the father of lies and the root of all sin, is by turning to the truth of God and his forgiveness.

Christ the only Just One, driven by "the Spirit . . . out into the wilderness" (Mark 1:12), is subjected to temptation so that sin can be conquered and man saved. He calls us to follow him in the battle for humanity's redemption: "The cup that I drink you will drink; and with the baptism with which I am baptized, you will be baptized," he says to his apostles (Mark 10:39). But he alone can support them in this ordeal of the Passion which is beyond their strength to bear.

He tells us this so that we may be comforted when we are tempted: "Simon, Simon, behold, Satan demanded to have you, that he might

sift you like wheat, but I have prayed
for you that your faith may not fail;
and when you have turned again,
strengthen your brethren" (Luke
22:31-32).

« 21 »

Christ is always with you in your struggle with temptation

"And when the devil had ended every temptation, he departed from him until an opportune time" (Luke 4:13). But from that moment, just after his forty days in the desert, until Gethsemane, Christ is continuously confronted by the Tempter.

Certain scribes and Pharisees, trying to provoke a charge on which they can arrest Jesus, set "traps" for him. In the language of the gospels, they are "testing" him. The same

Greek word is used for "test" in these passages, as is used for "temptation" in the "Lord's Prayer." It is instructive to look more closely at some of the examples of Jesus' being "tested."

In order to "test" him in his human condition as the Messiah, the Pharisees and Sadducees ask Jesus "to show them a sign from heaven" (Matthew 16:1).

When he is asked, "Is it lawful to divorce one's wife for any cause?" (Matthew 19:3), Jesus, the Word of God, is placed in contradiction with the law of God, and is thus being "tested" by his interlocutors.

"Why put me to the test, you hypocrites?" Jesus exclaims in response to the question about paying taxes to Caesar (Matthew 22:18). It has been designed to force the Messiah of Israel to confuse divine royalty with political royalty, the will to power.

In the same chapter (22:35ff.), a lawyer wanting to test Christ's faithfulness to the absolute love of God asks, "Teacher, which is the great commandment in the law?"

There are many other examples, including two described by John: Jesus' "testing" of Philip before he multiplies bread for the multitude who have followed him up the mountain (6:6), and the "test" to see whether Jesus will condemn the woman caught in the act of adultery (8:4ff.).

Thus, as he journeys up to Jerusalem, teaching as he goes and knowing that his Passion is imminent, Jesus is experiencing the explicit spiritual combat of temptation.

* * *

The greatest temptation, however, is to obstruct the plan of redemption. The point is vigorously emphasized by Jesus at Caesarea Philippi when, just after Peter has recognized Jesus as the Messiah and revolted against Jesus' announcement of his Passion, Jesus exclaims, "Get behind me, Satan! You are a hindrance to me; for you are not on the side of God, but of men." (See Matthew 16:21ff.)

In his prayer and spiritual struggle on the Mount of Olives, Jesus takes upon himself the condition of tempted man, and he delivers him from sin. Mercifully, he urges the disciples who have failed their "test" to stay awake: "Watch and pray that you may not enter into temptation" (Matthew 26:41).

Yes, let us dare to pray to our Father, "Keep us from entering into temptation."

In doing so, we can be assured that we are supported by Christ since he "in every respect has been tempted as we are" and is yet without sin, "For because he himself has suffered and been tempted, he is able to help those who are tempted" (Hebrews 4:15 and 2:18).

"In time of temptation," there is only one way to avoid falling away like seed which have failed to take root on rocky soil (Luke 8:13): we must pray and participate in the sacramental life, in union with Christ. This is no magic recipe, far from it. It requires us to come to grips with the hard fact that temptation is a spiritual combat.

In Christ, God gives us the strength to engage in this combat. Christ has unmasked our unique Adversary, the Tempter of human freedom. Moreover, he gives us the means of victory, as the Apostle Paul reminds the "rough" Christians at the port of Corinth: "No temptation has overtaken you that is not common to man. God is faithful, and he will not let you be tempted beyond your strength, but with the temptation will also provide the way of escape, that you may be able to endure it" (1 Corinthians 10:13).

Regardless of your weakness and your temptation (alcohol, hate, adultery, theft, despair), you are most likely thinking that you are fighting against yourself. You are mistaken.

In fact, you are fighting against something far stronger than you are. You may also think that you are alone with your weakness, your shame. You are mistaken again. You are with Christ who is doing battle for you.

To keep yourself from temptation, let Christ battle for you, with you. Open your heart, and hear the words he keeps repeating, ". . . be of good cheer, I have overcome the world" (John 16:33).

« **22** »

'But deliver us from evil'

The final request of the "Lord's Prayer" is the perfect complement to the preceding one. To understand it, we should look more closely at the two key words: "evil" and "deliver (us)."

Evil. In both Greek and Latin the word for evil designates either an abstraction or a person. Evil with a capital E, that is, the devil. This ambiguity, which does not exist in French or English, makes it crucial not to exclude either one of the meanings. To keep only the first would imply a surprising naïveté in the face of the "mystery of lawlessness"

(2 Thessalonians 2:7) so prevalent in the human condition.

Which evil, then, is Christ referring to in his prayer? Evil in all its depth and breadth: the evil from which God delivers us, the Evil One from whose hands he snatches us.

* * *

Is it possible that evil is a purely negative notion which expresses the absence of a good? Surely it is a reality which lashes our flesh, our hearts, and our spirits. Evil is all the suffering, all the aggression, all the wounding of human life — whether the cause be exterior circumstances or the wickedness of men. This kind of evil provokes a spontaneous cry of indignation and pain which is already a prayer: "O heavenly Father, deliver us. . . ."

But even worse is the evil which tempts us and whose accomplices we become. It would be a mistake to measure its damage from a purely personal point of view: "I'm angry with myself for having done that" or "I can't help it, that's the way I am" or by finding ways to excuse ourselves. We are not isolated in confronting evil. As human persons, we are constantly being caught in a double relationship: with other human beings and with God. Remember that the commandments which apply to ourselves are only the consequences of the commandments applying to our relations with God and our neighbor.

We have been given the freedom to turn away from God, and we can make choices which disregard his will and, hence, harm others and ourselves. In short, by our sins, we are in league with evil and are its partners in the destruction of the world and the wrenching or severing of bonds among its inhabitants.

* * *

However, behind the vast morass of evil there looms a power which is an absolute refusal of God. God has triumphed over that power, but man becomes its prisoner and its collaborator.

Our vision of evil tends to be too "hygenic," too "prophylactic," as if, just as in times of epidemics, it would suffice to cordon off a neutral zone where man could be protected from all contagion and personal complicity! Something in the character of evil has escaped us: its absurdity, its incomprehensibility. Otherwise, how can it happen that men and women, created by God for communion and holiness, destroy themselves? How has the world, created for beauty and peace, arrived at such a contradiction?

Some people denounce certain "systems," which the most desperate want to destroy. Actually, what a generation attributes to the "system" ought to be attributed to the devil. As Jesus teaches us, "This kind cannot be driven out by anything but prayer and fasting" (Mark 9:29).

We should make no mistake about who the enemy is. This perverse structure which we face is a *power*, "the power of darkness" (Luke 22:53; see also Colossians 1:13), who can be called by name: the Sly One, the Tempter, Satan.

The day before he suffers, Jesus, in the company of his disciples, turns to his Father and says, "I do not pray that thou shouldst take them out of the world, but that thou shouldst keep them from the evil one" (John 17:15).

And the Apostle Paul writes to the first Christian communities, ". . . the Lord is faithful; he will strengthen you and guard you from evil" (2 Thessalonians 3:3; see also 2 Timothy 4:18).

* * *

Our request, "Deliver us from evil," thus includes the evil which dwells in the hearts of men and the evil of the world — suffering and sin. And it reaches down to the source of evil, Satan the Tempter. In the end, therefore, to be delivered from evil is to be delivered from the devil, the apogee of cunning and subtlety.

((23))

Labor for the deliverance of humanity

"Deliver us from evil." The deliverance which we ask for is commensurate with the evil from which we ask to be freed. Christ has gone before us.

• Suffering. Just as Christ prayed on the Mount of Olives, "My Father, if it be possible, let this cup pass from me. . ." (Matthew 26:39).

• Regret, disappointment. "How often would I have gathered your children together as a hen gathers her brood. . ." (Matthew 23:37).

• Dread of death. When Christ

weeps for his friend Lazarus, he is experiencing in advance his own imminent death (cf. John 11:1-35).

- The ordeal of man tempted by and forced to contend "against the principalities, against the powers, against the world rulers of this present darkness, against the spiritual hosts of wickedness in the heavenly places" (Ephesians 6:12). It was the same for Christ in the desert. We pray, "Deliver us from evil," so that we may be protected from illusory fascination and remain capable of exercising our freedom while there is still time — because the first ruse of the Tempter is to conceal himself. And once we are on the narrow descending track of temptation, the horizon is no longer visible. The more we sink into the seduction of evil, the less space we have to move, the less strength to resist, the less judgment to distinguish between good and evil: "Fair is foul, and foul is fair," chant the witches in *Macbeth*. When we ask God's deliverance from evil, we are already identifying the devil behind the evil.

• The ultimate temptation of despair and abandon. When the time for Jesus' Passion comes, the apostles run away and Peter denies him three times. Judas, caught in the trap of Christ's death brought about by his betrayal, does not understand that the cross is the source of his deliverance. He succumbs to despair and takes his own life. And yet, Christ died for him, too.

* * *

Authentic liberation theology has its roots in this request of the "Lord's Prayer." The Father, by his Son, Redeemer of mankind, delivers us from the servitude of the Adversary — Satan — in order to grant us the freedom of children of God (cf. Matthew 17:26). Christ says to his disciples, ". . . you will know the truth, and the truth will make you free" (John 8:32).

After telling the parable

of the unrighteous judge and the importunate widow, Jesus asks a surprising question which reflects the extent and power of the devil from which we ask our Father to deliver us: ". . . when the Son of man comes, will he find faith on earth?" (Luke 18:8). It is faith which gives us the courage to watch and pray, to conquer Evil with the power of Love. Remember these other words of Jesus: "And because wickedness is multiplied, most men's love will grow cold. But he who endures to the end will be saved" (Matthew 24:12-13).

By our constant prayer, then, we join Christ's combat with evil, a combat which he will continue to wage until he comes in glory.

* * *

"Deliver us from evil" is a prayer which touches our concrete situation today as well as the ultimate fulfillment of God's plan at the end of time. Far from being an egotistical request for protection — "Lord, keep me out of evil's way" — it leads us to an active participation in Christ's labor for the liberation of all humanity.

Note that we say, "Deliver *us*," although it is you or I, as an individual, who is praying. To whom does "us" refer? To ourselves, certainly; to those who are dear to us; to the members of the Church. But we do not to stop there: we are also praying for *all of humanity*. Since we have been baptized, we are praying through, with, and in Christ, priest of all mankind. We are carrying out the sacerdotal function of God's people. Even the little child who stumbles through the "Lord's Prayer" is doing his part.

United with Christ, dead and resurrected, we are working for a deliverance whose price of sacrifice and strength of victory we know. Accused of being utopians, exposed to the "What good will it do?" attitude of the skeptics, we nevertheless continue, with the tenacity of waves striking the shore, to intercede for all humanity. When we pray, "Deliver *us* from evil," united with "his elect, who cry to him day and night" (Luke 18:7), we are working for the coming of the kingdom of God.

((24))

'For the kingdom, the power, and the glory are yours, now and forever'

The final effusion of praise in the "Lord's Prayer" is not an innovation of the Second Vatican Council. On the contrary, it is very old and probably dates back to the time of Jesus. The *Didache*, or Doctrine of the Apostles (second century), attests that it was already being used in the Christian communities of Israel, albeit in a slightly different form: "For thine is the power and the glory for ever and ever." The *Didache* adds the injunction: "Pray in this way three times a day" — which means in addition to the prayers at the temple. This instruction illustrates the liturgical character of the "Lord's Prayer." It is not at all a prayer improvised by Jesus for his disciples. The expressions are fashioned for his personal prayer, but according to the traditions of Jewish liturgical piety.

Jesus gives us the grace of sharing his omnipotent prayer, which is a summary of all prayer. When we pray with him, we enter into the perfect offering of the only Son. That is why we say it just before receiving his eucharistic body.

* * *

It would be strange and hardly conform to the logic of the prayer if it ended with the expression "Deliver us from evil" and the power of the Evil One. It would hardly seem appropriate to emphasize these words with an "Amen" which is, after all, the liturgical acclamation of God (see, for example, Revelation 5:14, 7:12, and 19:4). But the praise which attributes to God ". . . the power and the glory" and "the kingdom" whose advent we have asked for at the beginning of the prayer, finishes it off on a spontaneous note of thanksgiving which is customary in Jewish liturgy. Jesus confides precise words to his apostles for the prayer, but he invites them to conclude it by a completely free act of thanksgiving. The requests, for which the forms are fixed, have been made; now is the time for a more or less improvised expression of praise, a cry from the heart. This, at least, is the hypothesis that the exegetist Jeremiah has put forward to explain the lack of precision in ancient manuscripts containing this final expression of praise.

The kingdom

"You are our king, O Lord, our Father, the king of the world and of the children of God. You have manifested your sovereign goodness in sending your Son and your Holy Spirit. In your Son, you make of man a hereditary prince, king, and priest of creation."

By saying along with Jesus, who alone can express them in their plenitude, the words "thine is the kingdom," we are fulfilling the sacramental role of God's people. The author of the Book of Revelation reveals in a song to the Lamb the astonishing reality to which we are called: ". . . thou wast slain and by thy blood didst ransom men for God from every tribe and tongue and people and nation, and hast made them a kingdom and priests to our God, and they shall reign on earth" (5:9-10).

The power

"God, you are the almighty." Even if we extol the Father with distress and tears over the universal weakness which marks human existence, we are acknowledging, nevertheless, that God is infinitely omnipotent.

Through his Son, humiliated king to whom "all authority in heaven and on earth has been given" (Matthew 28:18), we participate in that sovereignty. We hear the echo of the promise Christ made to the apostles: ". . . you who have followed me will also sit on twelve thrones. . ." (Matthew 19:28). We are co-inheritors of the kingdom of God.

The glory

The plenitude of divine life bursts forth in the temple and is seen and described by Isaiah: ". . . I saw the Lord sitting upon a throne, high and lifted up; and his train filled the temple. Above him stood the seraphim; each had six wings: with two he covered his face, and with two he covered his feet, and with two he flew. And one called to another and said:

'Holy, holy, holy is the LORD of hosts; the whole earth is full of his glory' " (6:1-3).

We proclaim that this glory belongs to God, our Father. But, as sons and daughters in the Son, we shall have a part in it "when the Son of man comes in his glory" (Matthew 25:31) and his prayer is fulfilled: "Father, I desire that they also, whom thou hast given me, may be with me where I am, to behold my glory which thou hast given me in thy love for me before the foundation of the world" (John 17:24).

* * *

Our mission as the baptized is impressed like a watermark in this final outpouring of praise: we are always to act for the glory of God, we are to sanctify the world. Our world with its toughness must be kneaded by the powerful hands of God and transformed, like dough, by the blended yeast of the sons and daughters of God, the Church.

We are working so that the divine

power of love and salvation touches every event of human life and so that humanity, through our voices, gives thanks to the Father each time that we pray, "For the kingdom, the power, and the glory are yours, now and for ever."